CAPONE

Life Behind Bars at Alcatraz

Having finished about six-and-a-half years of an eleven-year term (almost four of them in Alcatraz), Chicago's No. 1 gangster, **Alphonse** ("Scarface") Capone, was reported to have gone berserk

From: "June" 2-21-38

Wide World

CONVICT CAPONE
Making beds?

on leaving the dining hall, to have been carried to the infirmary where he spent day after day foolishly making and unmaking his bed.

By Mark Douglas Brown

Golden Gate National Parks Conservancy
San Francisco, California

Published by
Golden Gate National Parks Conservancy
Bldg. 201 Fort Mason
San Francisco, CA 94123
(415) 561-3000
www.parksconservancy.org

The Golden Gate National Parks Conservancy
is a nonprofit membership organization created
to preserve the Golden Gate National Parks,
enhance the experiences of park visitors, and
build a community dedicated to conserving the parks for the
future. Your purchase of this publication helps support the
national parks at the Golden Gate.

Photographs in this book are from a variety of institutions and
private collections, and are included with the permission of the
individuals/archives from which they originate. Photo credits
appear with each image; for further information, please contact
the source.

The author wishes to extend a special thanks to the staff of the
National Archives and Records Administration, Pacific Region,
San Bruno, California.

ISBN-10: 1-883869-81-1, ISBN-13: 978-188386981-6
Library of Congress Control Number: 2003111869

Editors: Ruth T. Brown and Susan Tasaki
Design/Concept: Ruth T. Brown
Design/Production: Vickie Ho
Printed in Hong Kong

Cover: In May 1932, on his way to Atlanta to begin serving his eleven-year sentence
for income tax evasion, Capone smokes a cigar and smiles for newspaper
photographers. (© Bettmann/CORBIS)
Inside front cover: Capone with his attorney, 1929. (Chicago Historical Society)
Page 1: Al Capone (at left, in white fedora) walking down a Chicago street, ca. 1930.
(Chicago Historical Society)
Inside back cover: Capone, ca. 1933. (Getty Images)

Almost three thousand documents are known to exist from the prison life of Al "Scarface" Capone.

Incarcerated in 1932, the notorious gangster spent almost seven years in federal prisons: two at Atlanta Federal Penitentiary in Georgia; four at Alcatraz, the infamous island prison in San Francisco Bay; and just under one year at Terminal Island, in Long Beach, California. Released in November 1939, Capone spent the remaining years of his life at his mansion near Miami, Florida. He died in 1947 at age 48.

This book uses contemporary materials to trace Capone's life, revealing the personal experiences of a man who was a legend in his own time. Each document is authentic, scanned directly from the original files once held by the Bureau of Prisons, then lost for a time, and now at the National Archives in San Bruno, California.

The result is an inside look at Capone's prison years. From rap sheets, discipline reports, and anonymous threats to family letters, fan mail, and psychiatric assessments, these documents speak for themselves.

The story of Al Capone's rise to power in the Chicago underworld of the 1920s is legendary.

Alphonse Gabriel Capone was the fourth of nine children born to an immigrant Italian family in New York. His father ran a combination pool hall/bowling alley/barber shop; his mother took in sewing and cared for the family's coldwater walkup flat near the Navy Yard in the slums of Brooklyn. In his prison records, Capone says he left school at age 14 and went to work in a box factory where his childhood sweetheart, Mae Coughlin, also worked. Al and Mae were married in 1918, just after the birth of a son, Albert Francis, called by his nickname, "Sonny."

After Sonny's birth, Al took a job as a bouncer at a New York nightclub and brothel. There, some say, he was knifed over a passing insult to a woman, earning him the three slash marks that gave him his nickname, "Scarface." Though Capone was known to tell the press he'd received his scars fighting in World War I, prison documents record the more realistic claim that they were actually from fighting in his youth, and that he'd "sent the other guy to the hospital."

Capone married his childhood sweetheart Mary "Mae" Coughlin (above, ca. 1920) in 1918. They had one son, Albert Francis, called "Sonny," shown here with Al in 1928.

Al had to grow up fast on the tough streets of Brooklyn.

As a boy, he'd belonged to various gangs, and by the age of 18 had become acquainted with many of the underworld figures who would prove to be influential in his adult life. But it was what happened as he turned 21 that marked the real turning point of Al Capone's life: At midnight on January 16, 1920 — the night before his 21st birthday — prohibition went into effect, making the sale of alcohol illegal in the United States.

Like others, Capone knew it wasn't going to be easy for Americans to give up the beer, wine, and whisky they had once freely enjoyed. There would be great profits to be made by anyone who could supply these beverages to the drinking public. He could not have known, however, that his name would become synonymous with efforts to bring the public their forbidden drinks. Nor could he have known the power and fortune this venture would bring.

| Johnny Torrio

| "Big Jim" Colosimo

In 1919, Al found himself in big trouble.

He'd become embroiled in a fight that left a man from a rival gang near death. With the help of local underworld figure Frankie Yale, Capone left New York and went to Chicago, where he joined his old friend (and godfather to his son), Johnny Torrio. There, both men worked at Colosimo's, a popular Chicago nightclub established by "Big Jim" Colosimo.

Colosimo ran a profitable establishment. He was politically well-connected and knew many of Chicago's most influential people. But to the great irritation of his underlings, he seemed uninterested in the new bootlegging businesses of the day. Colosimo's shortsightedness, however, didn't last long. On May 11, 1920, he was gunned down in his nightclub — murdered, some say, by Frankie Yale.

After Colosimo's death, his crime connections were taken over by Johnny Torrio, who expanded his prostitution and white slavery rings and added new business ventures in gambling, alcohol sales, and protection rackets.

Opposite, in this 1930 souvenir photo, Al shares a beer with attorney J. Fritz Gordon (left) and Havana Mayor Julio Morales (right), at the Tropical Garden in Havana, Cuba. Right, the Capone family home at 7244 Prairie Avenue, Chicago, 1929.

This 1938 photo of Al Capone's custom-built armored Cadillac doesn't show the car's special features: steel-lined body, one-half-inch-thick bulletproof windows, and an engine capable of carrying the 8,000-pound vehicle at speeds of over 110 MPH.

By the early 1920s, there was tough competition for control of Chicago's bootlegging and crime industries. Gang murders were common, and Torrio, who had built a prosperous business, was a prime target for elimination. On January 24, 1925, he was ambushed and shot by rival gang leader George "Bugs" Moran. Remarkably, Torrio survived. But after recovering from multiple gunshot wounds, he decided to retire to Italy, leaving a thriving crime organization to his 26-year-old second-in-command, Al Capone.

Capone took over Torrio's gang in interesting times. It was the middle of the Roaring Twenties, the time of raccoon coats, bathtub gin, and brash young women called flappers.

Jazz became popular, and attitudes on many subjects, including sexuality and morals, began to loosen. The public enjoyed breaking the law, taunting officials by going to taverns and restaurants called speakeasies, where they could buy their illegal drinks and enjoy a forbidden night out on the town.

The lawless spirit of the times made Capone a celebrity.

Well-dressed and flamboyant, he was comfortable with the press. He held interviews and news conferences, and became noted for such quotes as "You can go a long way with a smile; you can go a lot farther with a smile and a gun," and "Vote early and vote often."

Above, Capone opened this Depression-era soup kitchen in 1931. The sign over the door reads "Free Soup, Coffee & Doughnuts for the Unemployed." Below, Chicago Cubs slugger Leo "Gabby" Hartnett signs a baseball for Sonny Capone during a charity game in 1931. Flanking Sonny are dad Al (right) and Frank "The Enforcer" Nitti (left), a key member of Capone's Gang

Capone's crime connections were public knowledge, but he carefully honed an image that the public liked; after all, he brought them their booze, and they were grateful for that. During the Depression, Capone even opened free soup kitchens to feed the poor.

Despite the embarrassment of federal officials, Capone appeared in newspapers and magazines, officiated at public events, was cheered when he took his seat at baseball games, and in March 1930, even made the cover of *TIME* magazine. To this day, Al Capone is probably the most recognized criminal in all the world.

Capone's rise to the top of the criminal heap was not only a testament to his business sense, but also to his brutality.

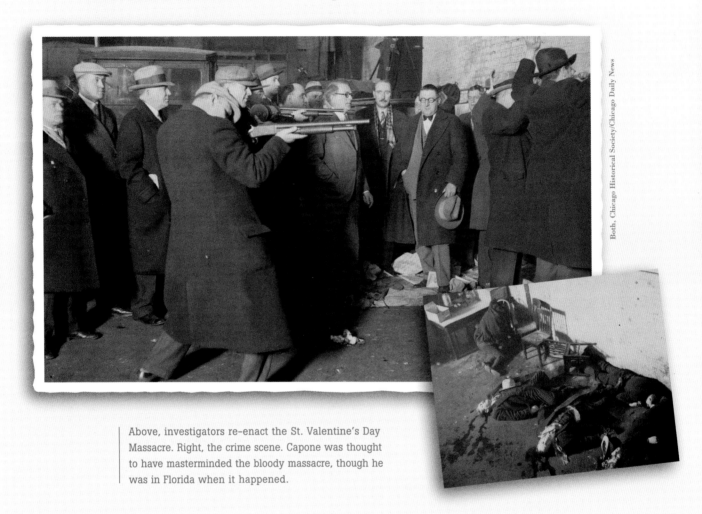

Above, investigators re-enact the St. Valentine's Day Massacre. Right, the crime scene. Capone was thought to have masterminded the bloody massacre, though he was in Florida when it happened.

Hundreds of murders were attributed to Capone and his men, including Chicago's bloody St. Valentine's Day massacre. On February 14, 1929, gangsters dressed as police officers fooled members of Bugs Moran's gang into believing their warehouse was being raided. The fake policemen lined up seven of Moran's men against a wall, and shot them — first with machine guns, and then with shotguns.

The public was outraged. Bugs Moran, who had just missed being among those murdered, told reporters "only Capone killed like that," and most believed him. Even though Capone was in Florida on the day of the killings, it was generally understood that such an event could not have taken place without his approval.

The violence continued, but people were getting tired of gangsters killing one another in the streets. Once titillating and exciting, Chicago was beginning to look too much like a lawless town.

MR. MITCHELL
WHY DONT YOU WAKE UP YOU
ARE HALF DEAD AND DONT
KNOW IT PLEASE DO SOMETHING
TO MAKE THE DECENT PEOPLE
PROUD OF YOU. YOUR DEPT. IS
THE LAUGHING STOCK OF ALL THE
WORLD AND A HUG FOR
ALL THE CROOKS THAT
AL CAPONE IS FREE
AGAIN WHY DONT YOU
ARREST HIM AND SEND
HIM TO THE ELECTRIC
CHAIR TO DEPORT HIM
TO ITIALY IS TO GOOD
FOR HIM. I KNOW HIM
VERY WELL HE IS A
MENACE TO THE WORLD
HE IS GUILTY OF NEARLY

Dated March 20, 1930, this anonymous note was sent to William D. Mitchell, Attorney General of the US. Above, Capone shakes hands with John Stege, a captain in the Chicago Police Department; above right, Capone poses in striped scarf, occasion unknown.

ALL THE KILLING OF
ALL THE CHIC GANGSTERS
IN CHICAGO AND ALL
THE BIG CITIES.
HE MAKES A BOAST TO
HIS PALS THAT ALL
THE POLICE AND
FEDERAL DEPT. ARE
AFRAID OF HIM.
ANY ONE WHO DIRECTS
A MURDER IS AS
GUILTY AS THE ONE
WHO DOES IT CAPONE
DIRESTS ALL THE
KILLING IN HIS GANG.
HE IS GUILTY I KNOW
KNOW WELL OF THE
TERRIBLE ST VALENTINE
MURDERS IN CHICAGO
FROM
(ONE WHO KNOWS.)

Getty Images

Capone had been adept at avoiding the law. Despite a litany of arrests, indictments, and fines, the only time he'd spent in jail was after the St. Valentine's Day massacre, when he was imprisoned in Philadelphia for carrying a concealed weapon.

Conveniently, the year Capone spent in Pennsylvania's Eastern State Penitentiary shielded him from retribution for the St. Valentine's Day killings without stopping his day-to-day business dealings.

Newspaper articles reported that a lenient system allowed Capone to furnish his spacious cell with elegant furniture, plush carpets, and paintings. Even from prison, Capone made a mockery of the law.

Above, a 1928 Miami mug shot; Capone was arrested for "suspicion" and released. Below, a modern recreation of Capone's cell at Pennsylvania's Eastern State Penitentiary based on a 1929 account from the *Philadelphia Daily Ledger*. The article, which may or may not have been accurate, probably added to the suspicion that Capone received special privileges.

By 1930, the federal government was fighting crime with the new laws of tax evasion.

Chicago Historical Society/Chicago Daily News

A confident Capone and lawyers convene at his 1931 tax-evasion trial; fearing foul play, the judge switched juries at the last minute.

In 1927, the Supreme Court had ruled that income, even income gained illegally, was subject to taxation. By proving that Capone owed back taxes — on his illegal as well as his legal profits — the courts finally found a way to pin him down. In 1931, Capone was sentenced to ten years in federal prison for income tax evasion, plus one additional year for contempt of court and perjury.

Ultimately, the Internal Revenue Service was able to do what the police could not. Legendary crime fighter Eliot Ness had accumulated enough evidence to prosecute Capone for violating prohibition laws, but government officials decided they had a better chance of winning their case by charging Capone with tax evasion. Ness, who never had the opportunity to confront Capone in court, went on to become Director of Public Safety in Cleveland, Ohio.

On May 4, 1932, Al Capone was incarcerated at Atlanta Penitentiary.

With his arrival came a blizzard of mail from well-wishers, news hounds, autograph seekers, and eccentrics.

Department of Justice
UNITED STATES PENITENTIARY
Atlanta, Georgia

Received .... MAY 4 1932 ....
From .. N - Ill. - Chicago ....
Crime Vio Income Tax Laws
Sentence: .. 10 .. yrs. ..—.. mos. ..—.. days
Date of sentence .... Oct 24 - 1931
Sentence begins .... May 4 - 1932
Sentence expires .... May 3 - 1942
Good time sentence expires Jan 19 - 1939
Date of birth 1-17-99 Occupation Gambler
Birthplace NY .... Nationality ....
Age 33 .... Comp. Med fr.
Height 5'-10½" ..... Eyes Gry
Weight 255 .... Hair Dk brn
Build Stout
Residence Chicago, Ill

Scars and marks b sc 4" across cheek 2" ot L ear - Vert sc 2½" on L jaw - b sc 2½" - 2" L ear on neck

CRIMINAL HISTORY

NAME	NUMBER	CITY	DATE	CHARGE	DISPOSITION
		NY City	1919	Dis Cond	Discharged
		Chicago Ill	1923	Traffic Vio	Dismissed
		Do	5-8-24	Murder Witness	Released
		Do	6-7-26	Vio N P A	Dismissed
		Do	1-28-26	Murder	Charge Withdrawn
		Do	10-1-26	Vio N P A	Dismissed
		Do	11-12-27	Refusal to Testify	Do
		Joliet Ill	12-22-27	Con. Weap	Fined 2600.00
		Phila. Pa	5-17-29	Con. Weap	Served 12 mos
		Miami Fla	1928	Susp.	Released
		Do	5-8-30	Do	Held 1 nights release

form ...... 66-12-9-31 5-M for other arrests see Declaration

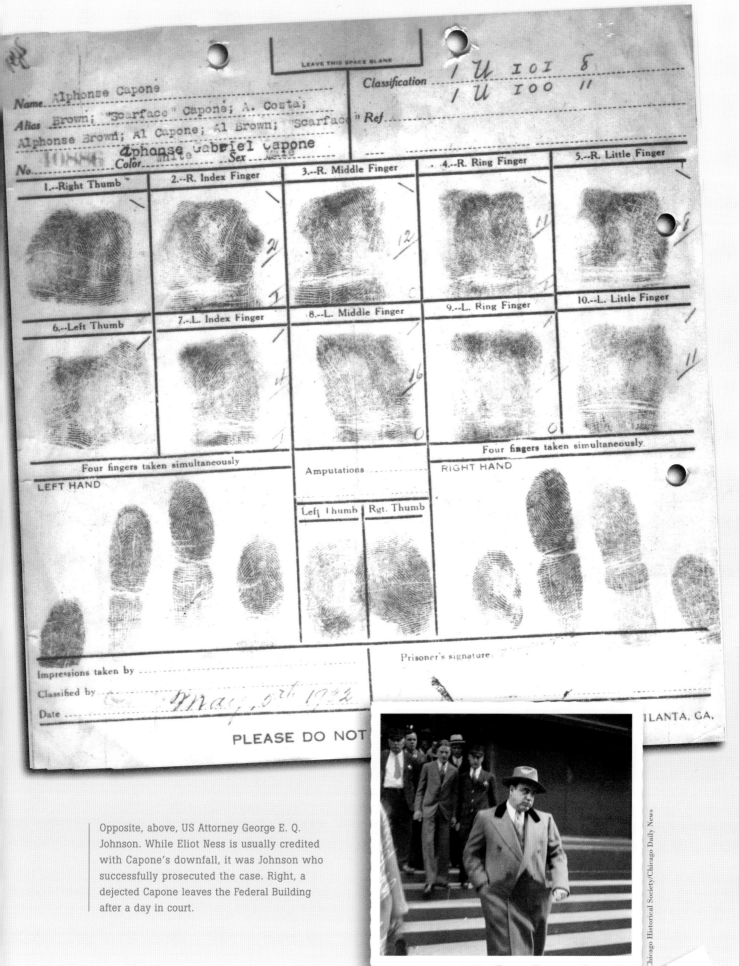

Name Alphonse Capone

Alias Brown; "Scarface" Capone; A. Costa; Alphonse Brown; Al Capone; Al Brown; "Scarface" Alphonse Gabriel Capone

No. 10886 Color White Sex Male

Classification 1 U IOI 8 / 1 U IOO 11

Ref.

LEAVE THIS SPACE BLANK

| 1.--Right Thumb | 2.--R. Index Finger | 3.--R. Middle Finger | 4.--R. Ring Finger | 5.--R. Little Finger |
| 6.--Left Thumb | 7.--L. Index Finger | 8.--L. Middle Finger | 9.--L. Ring Finger | 10.--L. Little Finger |

Four fingers taken simultaneously
LEFT HAND

Amputations

Left Thumb | Rgt. Thumb

Four fingers taken simultaneously
RIGHT HAND

Impressions taken by

Classified by

Date May 5th 1932

Prisoner's signature

ATLANTA, GA.

PLEASE DO NOT

Opposite, above, US Attorney George E. Q. Johnson. While Eliot Ness is usually credited with Capone's downfall, it was Johnson who successfully prosecuted the case. Right, a dejected Capone leaves the Federal Building after a day in court.

Above, a political cartoon pokes fun at the government's inability to control Capone and his gang. Below, people crowd the streets outside the Federal Building, where Capone's trial was taking place.

40886- Capone, Alphonse   May 18, 1932.

NEURO-PSYCHIATRIC EXAMINATION

FAMILY HISTORY

Paternal

Grand-Father: Gabrial Capone, died at a very old age, cause not known.

Grand-Mother: Theresa Capone, Died at a very old age, cause not known.

SIBLINGS

Father: Gabrial, died of hart trouble at the age of 55. Barber.

Uncle: Name not known, killed while in active service with the
         Italian Army.

Maternal

Grand-Father: Ralph Riola, dead, cause not known.

Grand-Mother: Theresa Riola, dead, cause not known.

SIBLINGS

Mother: Theresa Riola Capone, Age 68, living and in good health.

There was seven children in his mother's family, five boys,
two girls. He states that his mother exchanges correspondence with
her relatives in Italy, but he has no knowledge concerning the status
of the family.

He states the family history is negative as to insanity, tuberculosis,
cancer, suicide, syphilis and consanguinity.

The families, both paternal and maternal, were natives of Italy. He has been
informed that they were engaged in the business of buying, selling and expor-
ting Olive Oil. His father learned the barber profession, became self suppor-
ting and married at a very early age. Following the birth of the first child
he with his wife and child emigrated to this country, entering at New York City.
He become engaged in operating a combination pool room, bowling alley and
barber shop, locating in Brooklyn, where with the exception of the first child,
the other members of the family were born. He was naturalized and living in
the State of New York at Brooklyn, when he died. Since the death of his father,
his mother and all other members of the family have been living at his home in
Chicago.

40886- Capone, Alphonse

FAMILY HISTORY CONTINUED

SIBLINGS   Brothers and Sisters

James: Left home twenty years ago to go West. He has not been
              heard from since; if living he would be 40 years old.

Raplh: Age 37, health good, married, 1 child. Engaged in the
              real estate business. He is at this time serving a three
              year sentence in the federal penitentiary at Lavenworth,
              for having violated the Income Tax Law.

Francis: Died as the result of gun shot wounds at the age of 32.
              He was employed in the circulation and distribution dep-
              artment of a local newspaper, and injured while making
              deliveries in a truck by some unknown person.

Alphonse: Age 33, prisoner.

Arminia: Died at birth, cause not known.

Mimi: Age 29, health good, single. Owner and manager of a garage,
              in Chicago.

Albert: Age 28, health good, single. Associated with his brother
              Mimi, in the garage business.

Mathew: Age 26, health good, married, 1 child. Engaged in the
              security business at Chicago.

Mafalda: Age 24, health good, married, 1 child.

PERSONAL HISTORY

He is the fourth member of the family of nine. Born at Brooklyn, N. Y.,
January 18, 1899. Normal birth and childhood. He states that he has no knowledge of having had childhood diseases. Pneumonia at the age of 30. No other
adult illness. He has three scars on the face, residuals of injuries recieved
in a fight. Scar in groin, residual of bullet wound inflicted by an unknown
person. No other injuries. Began school at the age of 7 attended regularly and
reached sixth grade at 14. He states that he was interested in school and liked
to attend. He took part in all usual activities at school, and was considered
apt by his teachers, and relates of nothing out of the ordinary during childhood. He states that at the age of 12 he obtained work as a pin boy in a bowling
alley, working during vacation and after school hours. At the age of 14, he was
compelled to quit school to assist with the support of the family.

Capone talks about his family in this 1932 document. Note that Capone has lost track of his oldest brother, James. A noted marksman, James (Vincenzo) took the name of a silent-movie cowboy, and came to be known as "Two-Gun Hart." He served in WWI, married, had three sons, and in 1920, became a prohibition agent. James didn't contact his family again until 1940, when he needed financial help.

40886- Capone, Alphonse

PERSONAL HISTORY CONTINUED

He obtained employment in the production department of the United Paper Box Co., manufacturers of fancy paper and leather boxes. He states this class of work requires considerable skill and beginers were paid seven dollars a week. He was promoted to higher position and was receiving twenty three dollars a week when he resigned after serving seven years with the one company. At the age of 22 he accepted a position as manager of a dance hall in New York City. Six month later he resigned to accept a similiar position at Chicago. Here be became engaged in various business enterprises, including real estate, newspapers, hotels, garages, and security. He states that he has accumulated considerable money, and claims Chicago as his residence. He states that he ran away and married at the age of 17, his boyhood sweethart. They had attended school togather, and were working at the same factory when married. His wife was Mae Coughlin and 16 years of age when they married. There is one child, no miscarriges. Both wife and child are in good health and living at their home at Chicago. He contracted gonorrhea at the age of 24; treated and cured by a physician. In 1931 his blood Wasserman showed positive for which he was given several intramuscular, anti-luetic injections. He denies the use of drugs, admits the use of beer and wine. No military record. No compensation.

CRIMINAL HISTORY   (See attached report from Record Office)

He states that his arrests have been to numerous to mention, useing as a criterion the fact that he was arrested eight different times in twenty four hours at Miami, Florida.

- 1929- Arrested at Philadelphia, Pa., by city police charged with posession of a revolver. Pled guilty. Sentenced to serve one year in jail.

- 1931- Arrested at Chicago, by federal officers charged with having violated the Income Tax Law. Pled not guilty. Sentenced to serve ten years in this institution.

COMPLAINTS

Sinus trouble. Kidney trouble.

Al (second from left) leaves the courthouse after his trial.

DEPARTMENT OF JUSTICE
UNITED STATES PENITENTIARY
ATLANTA, GEORGIA

Date *June 22*

TO: *Leader of Orchestra*

SIR:—

Please grant me an interview regarding—

Request that I be given an opportunity to learn bass in the band. I promise to do my best to learn, so that I may be of use to the band. Thanking you in advance

Number *40886* Cell *3-7* Detail *Shoe Shop*

Name *Alphonse Capone.*

State briefly, exactly what you wish to discuss.
Do not use any other form.
Do not use an envelope.
Deposit this slip in the mail-box as you do your outgoing letters.
You will not be called unless your request merits consideration.

© Bettmann/CORBIS

DEPARTMENT OF JUSTICE
UNITED STATES PENITENTIARY
ATLANTA, GEORGIA

Date July 26th, 19_

TO:- Deputy Warden,

SIR:-

Please grant me an interview regarding—

My Wife sent to me five pictures of herself and my Baby all different poses and I was call and was informed that I could only receive one and that I would have to send the other four back home telling me that with your permission I would be allowed to have the other four. Sir rather than send them back and infere they may get lost. Sir if I am not allowed to have them wish you would send for me so I may have them distroyed in your presents as I dont want them go astray as some New's Paper may get them, Thanking you in advance.

NUMBER 40886 CELL 3-7 DETAIL Shoe Sho_

NAME *Alphonse Capone*

STATE BRIEFLY EXACTLY WHAT YOU WISH TO DISCUSS.
Do not use any other for_
Do not use an envelope
DEPOSIT THIS SLIP IN THE MAIL BOX AS YOU DO YOUR OUTGOING LETTERS.
YOU WILL NOT BE CALLED UNLESS YOUR REQUEST MERITS CONSIDERATION.

Al had two requests as he entered the penitentiary: one, permission to join the band and two, to destroy family photos so they didn't "go astray." Above right, Al and US Marshall Harry Laubenheimer play cards to pass the time aboard the prison train heading for the US Penitentiary in Atlanta.

BY DIRECT WIRE FROM
WESTERN UNION

CLASS OF SERVICE

This is a full-rate Telegram or Cablegram unless its deferred character is indicated by a suitable sign above or preceding the address.

NEWCOMB CARLTON, PRESIDENT   J. C. WILLEVER, FIRST VICE-PRESIDENT

as shown on all messages, is STANDARD TIME.

The filing time as shown in the date line on full-rate telegrams and day letters, and the time of receipt at destination

QN33 41 8 EXTRA=CD NEWYORK NY JUL 22 143P

WARDEN FEDERAL PENITENTIARY=

LONDON DAILY TELEGRAPH STATES CAPONE WRITING BOOK ON ADVICE

TO EVILDOERS STOP WOULD YOU BE GOOD ENOUGH INFORM ME IF THIS

TRUE AND IF CAPONE WILLING NEGOTIATE ENGLISH RIGHTS STOP

PLEASE REPLY COLLECT=

:RANDALL DAILY EXPRESS

235 EAST 45 STREET N

PATRONS ARE REQUESTED TO FAVOR THE COMPANY BY CR

CLASS OF SERVICE DESIRED

DOMESTIC	CABLE
TELEGRAM	FULL RATE
DAY LETTER	DEFERRED
NIGHT MESSAGE	NIGHT LETTER
NIGHT LETTER	WEEK END LETTER

Patrons should check class of service desired; otherwise message will be transmitted as a full-rate communication.

WESTERN UNION

NEWCOMB CARLTON, PRESIDENT   J. C. WILLEVER, FIRST VICE-PRESIDENT

CHECK

ACCT'G INFMN.

TIME FILED

Send the following message, subject to the terms on back hereof, which are hereby agreed to

Ans date   Atlanta, Ga., July 22, 1932.

Randall Daily Express Correspondent,   40886
235 East 45th Street, New York, N. Y.

Replying telegram. Have no knowledge that Al Capone is writing book
on advice to Evil Doers.

                              A. C. Aderhold,
                                  Warden.

COLLECT

Almost immediately, prison officials were besieged by requests from prominent people — from Congressmen to movie-makers — to interview Al Capone. A. C. Aderhold, warden of the Atlanta Federal Penitentiary, and Sanford Bates, director of the Bureau of Prisons, were bombarded with questions: Does Capone lounge around, conducting business-as-usual from behind bars? Does he have a phone in his cell? Does he really wear silk underwear and custom-made shoes?

August 1, 1932   SB :MAM

MEMORANDUM FOR THE DIRECTOR,
   BUREAU OF INVESTIGATION:

     Within the last two or three weeks there have come from various Members of Congress and other officials in widely separated parts of the east requests for various people to visit Prisoner Al Capone at Atlanta Penitentiary. Among others such requests have been forwarded to us from Senators Copeland, Senator Davis, Congressman Disney Congressman Ramspeck, Congressman Murphy and Congressman Bloom. In each instance the permission has been refused in a letter similar to one of those in the attached file.

     I reported this matter to Assistant Attorney General Youngquist, and he felt that it was possible that your Bureau might run down some of these requests to see what was behind it all.

                         Very truly yours,

                         Director.

JOHN EDGAR HOOVER
DIRECTOR

AP/Wide World

U. S. Department of Justice
Bureau of Investigation
Washington, D. C.

August 10, 1932.

CONTENTS NOTED
AUG 1 1 1932
S. B.

MEMORANDUM FOR THE DIRECTOR, BUREAU OF PRISONS.

     I beg to acknowledge receipt of your communication of August 1st, advising of the receipt by you of requests from various members of Congress and other persons, for permission to visit Al Capone at the Atlanta Penitentiary, said permission to be accorded certain individuals, mentioned in said requests.

     When possible so to do, without jeopardizing the current work of this Bureau in criminal investigations, I will arrange that inquiries be made along the lines indicated, confining such in-quiries, of course, to such as will not involve any embarrassment because of the official status of the persons from whom letters have been received.

     I am returning the original communications in question for your files.

                    Very truly yours,

                    J. Ce. Hoover

                    Director.

CAPONE CODDLED IN ATLANTA PRISON

Still 'Big Shot' and Wears Silk Underwear, Says Former Convict

HIS SHOES $25 A PAIR

Following is the first of a series of three stories describing Al Capone's life in Federal prison at Atlanta, where he is serving a sentence of 11 years for income tax fraud. The author is an ex-convict, committed from Philadelphia, who worked in the prison shoe shop with the notorious gang leader. He has just been released, after completing a sentence of 28 months for impersonating a Federal officer.

BY EX-CONVICT NO. 35,503

Atlanta, Ga., Jan. 23.—Al Capone remains "the big shot."

He was "the big shot" in the years he dominated Chicago's racketeering underworld and he is still "the big shot" behind the gray walls of Atlanta prison—at least so far as his personal comfort and special privileges are concerned.

Outside of actually being permitted to leave the walls, he gets about what he wants over there in the Big House, far more at any rate than the ordinary prisoner.

Plentifully supplied with money (although no other prisoner is permitted to have more than $10 at one time) he still wears the silk underwear that he boasts costs him $12 a suit, he wears suits tailored for him in the prison tailor shop and the specially made shoes that he says costs him $25 a pair.

Other convicts wear the regulation prison issue garb.

He receives and sends a voluminous mail, although other prisoners are limited to writing two letters a week. On the ground that it is "business correspondence" much of it goes uncensored. I've seen him get lots of uncensored letters.

In the matter of visitors, too, he gets a fairly free hand. They're coming down here all the time from Chicago to see him, and Al persuaded the authorities to let him have a special room in which to see them. There isn't any guard around when Al talks business with his friends.

His "work" in the shoe ship is more or less a joke. He usually shows up for an hour or two in the morning to tack on some rubber heels. Then there will be visitors, or he goes over to the hospital for treatment, or play tennis. He has special hours on the tennis court.

Often he spends nights in the hospital, where there are regular mattresses on the beds instead of the straw ticks used in the cells.

Sometimes he eats with the other prisoners. Sometimes he doesn't.

With his money, he can buy things from the commissary that are a good deal more appetizing than the prison grub, which isn't so hot.

But with all his money and his special privileges, Al Capone is a mighty unhappy man.

When he first came down to the prison, he cried on everybody's shoulder that would listen to him about how he had been "double-crossed" and "cheated" by the authorities in Chicago. He said he had distributed 300 "grand" in Chicago to insure a light sentence, but they crossed him up, he said.

I've heard him put his head in his hands and say, "Oh, why did I do it?" I don't know whether he meant the crime for which he was sentenced or the 300 "grand."

Naturally, getting all these privileges, and his perpetual crabbing against his fate and everything else hasn't tended to make him very popular with the other inmates. He has a small clique around him that toady to him for cigars, cigarettes, extra food, and other things that make life in there more endurable. The prison commissary even put in his own favorite brand of cigars. He buys them by the box.

They call him "Grease Ball" and "Wop" and "Macaroni Bender" and make obscene cracks about his being "a big shot."

And he will yell at them, "Shut up, you mugs, I've handled more dough than you and all your families ever saw," with plenty of profanity mixed up in it.

He has been trying for some time to wangle a transfer to the new Federal prison at Lewisburg, Pa. But he hasn't had much luck yet.—(©1933.)

Accusations by a disgruntled ex-con captivated readers and led to inquiries by the Bureau of Prisons (see p. 22 for the warden's official response). Above, Capone, ca. 1933.

These stories, circulated around the world, struck a chord with the public, who were fascinated with the notoriety of the crime czar.

In fact, prison officials and the Attorney General's office were also interested in the allegations. Capone's alleged privileges were criminal violations. If the charges could be proven, the government could lock up Al for a lot longer than the eleven years he'd already received. At the FBI, Director J. Edgar Hoover and his men diligently investigated but could not prove any of the rumors true.

DEPARTMENT OF JUSTICE

UNITED STATES PENITENTIARY

ATLANTA, GEORGIA

Office of the Warden

January 24, 1933.

Director, Bureau of Prisons,
Department of Justice,
Washington, D. C.

Dear Sir:

I wish to call attention to charges made by Ex-Convict No. 35503, who claims to have been released from this institution January 28, 1932, that Al Capone register No. 40886, is receiving special privileges in this institution. Answering the charges made I beg to advise as follows:

1. Is he permitted to go out of the prison at night?

No. This statement is absolutely false. He has only been out of the prison twice since his incarceration here May 4, 1932, and then to the United States Court in Atlanta.

2. Does he keep up a voluminous business correspondence?

No. No more than the regular prisoners. He has asked for only one special letter since his arrival.

3. Does he go to his job an hour or two late and then hang around?

No. He is absent from his work only on the Doctor's orders when taking a course of treatment as outlined in report of the Chief Medical Officer, Public Health Service, copy of which is enclosed.

4. Does he have special hours on the tennis court?

He has thirty minutes per day the same as the other men; that is from 3:25 to 3:55. During this time he can select his own exercise, pitching horse shoes, indoor baseball, tennis, or walking, as he chooses.

5. Does he ever spend the nights in the hospital?

He has been committed to the hospital on orders of the Doctor twice.

6. Does he have extra visits without a guard?

Positively no. On account of reports that his friends would probably try to smuggle money and guns to him, we have not been permitting his interviews to be held with other prisoners, but each interview is held in the present of an officer and where his movements could be watched and his conversations clearly heard.

7. Does he sometimes eat alone?

He eats his meals along with the other men in the regular dining room.

8. Is he permitted the use of all the money he wants to buy special articles from the commissary?

He can only spend $10.00 per month in the commissary. His account shows that he has withdrawn $97.00 since May 4, 1932. This covers $10.00 per month with the exception of December, when $5.00 extra is granted all prisoners, and he spent $2.00 in returning his clothing and a package to his home.

9. Did he have a special brand of cigars put in the commissary?

No. He has never made such a request.

10. Does he wear silk underwear?

No. This has been verified by his foreman and the Medical Officer in the United States Public Health Service, the Foreman stating that he has noticed his underwear from time to time and also noticed it this morning and that he had on the regulation underwear. The Medical Officer states that he has had occasion to strip him for examination, and he also states that he wears regulation underwear.

11. Does he wear special tailor made suits?

No. This is verified by his foreman, the Deputy Warden and the Medical Officer, U. S. Public Health Service.

12. Does he wear $25.00 shoes?

No. His foreman in the shoe shop says that he is wearing the regulation shoes manufactured in the Penitentiary Shoe Shop at Leavenworth, Kansas.

Capone, during his incarceration in this institution, has had no special favors not granted all other first grade prisoners. It was made clear to me by the officials in Washington, at the time Capone was committed to this penitentiary, that he could have absolutely no favors or special privileges not granted other prisoners, and these instructions have been carried out.

Yours very truly,

(Sgd.) A. C. ADERHOLD,

Warden.

| Capone (center) is escorted to Atlanta Federal Prison.

1933
Oct   31   INSOLENCE:
The above named prisoner was told by me to wash a window.
I assigned one window to each member of the detail;
everyone, including the above named man, washed their
window. After they xxxxx had completed their work, this
prisoner became very insolent and wanted a pass to the
Deputy Warden, saying that he would not wash windows for
anyone. This man created quite a bit of confusion amongst
the detail when he began yelling out "Did you see me wash
that window?". This is the second time this prisoner
has become insolent to me, in front of the other members
of the detail.

                                        Guard-- E.W.Yates.
ACTION: Reprimanded and warned.

April 26, 1933.

Mr. M. F. Peters,
Box 668,
Midland, Texas.

Dear Mr. Peters:

I have your letter of April 23, 1933, and
very much regret that under our rules it will be
impossible to permit Al Capone to sketch a cattle
brand for you. I am returning the papers which
you enclosed with your letter.

                          Yours very truly,

                          Director.

Form J A G 191   3M

DISCIPLINARY REPORT

UNITED STATES PENITENTIARY

Atlanta, Ga., 10- .... 19 ....

Name Capone

No. 40886 .... Cell 3-7 Employed Shoe Shop

Offense Too much underwear, socks & pillows.

Specifications. This clothing was put on this man's bed tied up with sheets & personal clothing. There was also eight (8) extra sheets on his bed.

J. G. Wright
                                        Guard

(over)

Action
Reprimanded and ....

                          { Writing ....
Privileges Taken { Tobacco ....
                          { Yard ....
                          { Amusement ....

Reduced to .... Grade

Placed in Isolation [Solitary] on restricted diet until he has
given promise of obedience.

....
....
....

                                        Deputy Warden

........................19 ...

Despite reassurances, some still believed that Capone
was receiving special privileges in Atlanta. That the
allegations had not been proved (and never were)
was no consolation. Prison administrators, no
doubt concerned that they were beginning to look
incompetent in the eyes of the public, realized that
if Capone were sent to Alcatraz, the new maximum-
security facility in San Francisco Bay, the situation
could be better controlled. Unlike other prisons,
inmates were not paroled directly from Alcatraz, so
it was harder for reporters to get fresh stories.

Mr. Warden, Dear Sir:

Time is passing swiftly and I am rapidly drawing near my four score yrars; and m y heart is crying out to meet Al Capone in the bright beyond.   No, he does not know me, never heard of me, yet I long to save him from future sorrows.

We are told in the holy writings that "he that converteth a soul covereth a multitude of sins"; and I so long to convert asoul.

When you have read his letter and yours, cut off my name and what follows and seal them up, so he cannot know who I am nor where I I live.until he is living a free and happy life.

North Webster, Indiana
March 26, 1934

Dear sir:
I am trying to make a collection of the signatures of well-known people. It would help me if you would be willing to have Al Capone sign his name at the bottom of this letter and mail it to me in the enclosed stamped and addressed envelope.
Thank you very much for this kind ness. Yours very truly,
Thomas K. Warner

JAG 82 3-33 50M

DEPARTMENT OF JUSTICE
UNITED STATES PENITENTIARY
ATLANTA, GA.

May 23, 34

Dr. Ossenfort
Sir:

Prisoner No. 40886 who is on Old and Crippled was engaged in a game of tennis this afternoon.

Respectfully,
M. Elliott
Yard Patrol

Mr Elliott:
This pt is convalescing from a fractured rt hand. He was advised to play tennis provided hand did not give too much pain. So not considered fit for duty yet —

Letters from the outside world poured into USP Atlanta, begging Capone for autographs, money, and favors. Some offered redemption; others, warnings and threats. Inside, Capone was struggling to adjust to life in prison, as these reports show.

25

August 22, 1934, Al Capone arrived at Alcatraz Penitentiary in San Francisco.

Curiously, there are no documents in Capone's files noting the reason for his transfer. Alcatraz was a maximum-security prison reserved for troublesome federal prisoners. Al had not been particularly troublesome, but his transfer probably made officials look as though they were taking control of his supposed antics.

DIVISION OF INVESTIGATION, U. S. DEPARTMENT OF JUSTICE
WASHINGTON, D. C.

Record from _U.S Penitentiary_ (Address) _Alcatraz, Cal_
On the above line please state whether Police Department, Sheriff's Office, or County Jail

Date of arrest _Aug 22, 1934_

Charge _No Income Tax_

Disposition of case _10 yrs_

Residence _Chicago, Ill_

Place of birth _Brooklyn, NY_

Nationality _Ital-American_

Criminal specialty _Hoodlum_

Age _35_ Build _Stocky_

Height _5-9_ Comp _DK_ Hair _Blk slight bald_

Weight _214_ Eyes _Brown_

Scars and marks _Lge ragged cut scar on left side of neck_

CRIMINAL HISTORY

NAME	NUMBER	CITY OR INSTITUTION	DATE	CHARGE	DISPOSITION OR SENTENCE
Alphonse Capone	40886	U.P. Atlanta Ga		(Transf to U.P. Alcatraz Cal 8-22-34)	

Opposite, Alcatraz correctional officer. Left, one of 53 convicts headed for Alcatraz from Atlanta, Capone traveled by prison train to Tiburon, California. There, the three railcars were rolled onto a barge and powered by tugboat to the island dock. No one was allowed off the train until it reached Alcatraz. Above, Al's receiving document — note his criminal specialty.

7244 Prairie Avenue
Chicago Illonois

December 3, 1934

Hon. Homer Cummings
Attorney-General United States
Washington, D.C.

Honorable Sir:

During all of the time my
son, Alphonse Capone, was incarcerated in
the Federal Prison at Atlanta, his wife and
myself were permitted to visit him in com-
pliance with the rules of that prison.

We desire to visit him at
the prison at which he is now confined,
namely, the Alcatraz, located in the Pacific
Ocean. We understand the rules of that prison
in respect to visitors are such as to make
it impossible to meet under the same conditions
which existed at Atlanta, Ga.

We respectfully request you
to exert your influence to enable us to visit
this prisoner as formerly, and to be accorded
the same privileges as existed at that time.
We trust that we are not, in this request, seeking
a special and forbidden privilege, and rely
upon your sense of fairness and humanity to
enable us to secure this privilege.

I remain,

Respectfully yours,

Theresa Capone

Mario Gomes Collection

Al's mother, Theresa Capone, in the back
yard of the family's Prairie Avenue home in
Chicago. Capone kept this photo with him
in his Atlanta prison cell.

28

In her December 1934 letter (opposite), Theresa Capone asks permission
to visit her son Alphonse at "the Alcatraz, located in the Pacific Ocean."
This photo, ca. 1945, shows the island's relationship to San Francisco,
and is approximately the view Mrs. Capone would have had.

Above, USP Alcatraz in the 1940s. Opposite, Mae Capone, who came to California to visit her famous husband, hides from cameras.

No. *85*

The holder of this card is allowed to have in his cell the articles listed here in addition to the articles authorized in Regulations.

Shuttleworth
DEPUTY WARDEN
By
Michelson

2 sets of music inst. books
1 full set of finger control music   W. F. P.
1 full Tenor banjo Course   W. F. P.
Music writing sheets   W. F. P.
ass. Copies of song   W. F. P.
1 worlds almanac "36"   W. F. P.
Family Pictures   W. F. P.
The Blessed Friend of Youth   W. F. P.
Seeing Italy Newman   W. F. P.

I

To My Dear Wife.   Feb.

     Well Sweet, here I am with a few lines to you, the dearest in all the world
to me. And have prayed these last few days of my sickness to our dear Godaabove to
make me well, and which she has, and I sure thanked her for making me well and sure
am in perfect health again, as you and Mafalada will see on your visiting days this
month. I also received all of your letters Sweet, and more then happy that you and
our dear Son, are in perfec t health, I also heard from my dear Sister and also
brother Ralph please give them my love, and also tell Ralph not to worry about me,
as I am in good health, and intend to be home, when my time is up, unless I have to
go to the County Jail in Cook County, Sweet I received this month two letters
dated Feb. 3 r - 5th, and sure enjoyed them and happy that you and Sonny and all the
rest of our dear familys are in good health give them all my love and kisses to the
kids and please dont worry about me, as you will see for your-self how I look when
you get here on visit with Mafalda, so keep that

lovely chin, up and remember Sweet, it isn't much longer before I will be home, and
into your loving arms forever, so Sweet don't worry about me as am O.K and will be
on routine working in the yard A.M and Music afternoon in no less than two more
days. So you see Sweet, nothing to keep you worried, as when you visit me, you will
see your-self Sweet, that your dear Dad is in good health. Give my love to Mother
and glad in Mafalda's letter she told me Mother is in perfect health and also the
rest our dear familys are the same, I thank God and pray night and mornings, to
keep up her good work. In the meantime tell Ralph notto worry about me, as all is
going to be in perfect shape, in regards my doing the rest of time, and come in
perfect health and dont intead to make any moves of any kind, outside of obeying
my officers and respecting them, and doing my work, so you see my dearest, there is
nothing for any of you to worry, smile and keep that smile until your dear dad
comes home, and then Sweet, watch me strut my tuff. and all my love and I mean
Sweets for you alone, and with heart and sole, and forever and ever. Sweet here's
my word to you, from a couple a days from now, I will be in perfect health and
intend to be in perfect health when I come home which is time is getting shorter
and shorter, until I see you and my dear sister, lease do not worry, then you will
be satisfied that I'm not in bad shape, as what you have heard. So chin up Sweet,
and remember, we goingto have plenty happiness ahead for us and our future, and
rest our lives, and Sweet remember this promise, nothing in this world is ever
goingto interefire with our future happiness, Sweet I mean this, and all I can
add to this promise is for you and dear Son and famlys all keep in perfect health,
and not worry about your dear dad, as nothing at is going to get your dear dad down,
in the meantime tell Sonny to up the way he is doing at Colledge and me as often
as he can, and kiss as often you can for me and God Bless all of you. Your dear
dad. Alphonse Capone #85
XXXXXXXXXXXXXXXXXXXXXXXXXXXXXXXXXXXXXXXXXXXXXXXXXXXXXXXXXXXXXXXXXXXXXXXXXXXXXXXXXXXXX

    The above letter written by Alphonse Capone #85
was addressed by him as follows:

     Mrs. Mae Capone
     93 Palm Island
     Miami Beach
     Florida

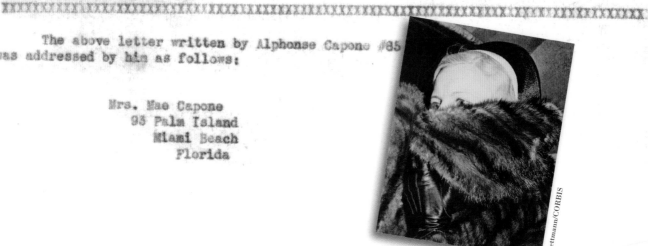

LIBRARY REPORT

Concerning the reading of the following inmate:
Alphonse CAPONE. #.85. , from the list of books drawn since,
June, 1st, 1935, on his library card, showing the general
trend of his reading matter, Viz :

425-A54.	Common Errors in English corrected. : Anderson.	
914.5-M45.	Fortnight in Naples.	Maure.
780-K62.	Rudiments of Music.	Kitson.
780-P51.	How to enjoy Music.	Reyser
720-K21.	American Home book of Building.	Kauffman.
635-C64.	Practical Flower Gardening.	Cloud.
308-R78.	Looking Forward.	F.D.Roosevelt.
910.4-S63.	Sailing alone around the world.	Slocum.Jr.
918.1-F59.	Brazilian. Adventures.	Fleming.
170-P68.	Life beguins at Forty.	Pitkin.

Inmates could select three books at a time
from the limited list of preselected and often
out-of-date books in the prison library (above).
Right, in the prison laundry, inmates cleaned
and pressed towels for the US Navy.

In his early days at Alcatraz, Al Capone, #85, was generally regarded as a good prisoner.

Records tell of one fight with a fellow inmate in the laundry room where they both worked. The guards quickly broke it up, and both were sent to solitary confinement for eight days. Otherwise, Capone committed no serious offenses.

NOTE: Early return of this form is requested. Under remarks the Board will appreciate any pertinent information that in your opinion may be of aid to them. Complete form for applicant who has been relieved from your supervision and state date and department transferred to.

CONFIDENTIAL WORK REPORT
to
THE UNITED STATES BOARD OF PAROLE

U. S. Penitentiary, Alcatraz, Calif.

Date __August 8,__ 193__5__.

NAME __Alphonse Capone__   REGISTER NO. __85,__

Department __Library__

Actual occupation in institution __Principally, Making out Book Cards.__

Approximate length of time under your observation __Ten weeks.__

Draw a line around the word or words that best fit his description in the following two questions:

How would you classify him as a worker?

EXCELLENT   (GOOD)   FAIR   POOR   VERY POOR

How would you classify him as to character?

Trustworthy	Grouchy	Slow
(Friendly)	Agitating	Lazy
(Pleasant)	Tricky	(Talkative)
(Energetic)	(Boastful) Somewhat	Defiant
(Faithful)	Excitable	Stubborn
Quarrelsome	Unreliable	Hot-headed
Skeptical		

REMARKS: __I have been pleasantly surprised at the attitude of__
__Alphonse Capone, Reg. No. 85, towards me and towards his work.__
__The only really objectionable thing about him, which I have noticed,__
__is a too great readiness upon his part to offer unasked advice, or__
__to make suggestions as to when or how things ought to be done.__
__Upon the whole, I would very much dislike to lose him from the__
__library force, if he remains in the Institution.__

Then, in May 1936, Ralph Capone, Al's older brother, received a letter from an ex-inmate at Alcatraz warning that Al's life was in danger. Before long, information from many sources, including the newspapers, began saying the same thing. Capone's attorney and family asked that Al be transferred to another institution, but James A. Johnston, warden of Alcatraz, and Sanford Bates, director of the Bureau of Prisons, assured everyone that Capone was safe at Alcatraz.

Above, "Seedy" (C-D) Street; when Capone first arrived, his cell was at the far left end on the second level. The prisoner on the right in this photo is standing close to the cell that housed Machine Gun Kelly at about the same time. Right, inmates line up in the recreation yard to be escorted to work details. Records show that Capone worked in the yard, library, laundry, and shower room.

May 18, 1936.

Dear Ralph:

This is pertaining to your brother Al now in Alcatraz, Calif. Enclosed you will find true statements in regards to the conditions that exist there at present. Upon arriving at the Island Al your brother was approached by the Touhy Bunch and others of his clicks to advance $5000 to be used as an escape plan to hire gun-boat and for people on the outside on threat of his life, which they have attempted time and time again for him refusing to advance same. A year or so ago this same bunch planted a table knife under his seat in dining room which would have caused him going to the hole and maybe lose his good time, which the Deputy Warden knew at time that Al could not have done it; a party by the name of Whaley working in the kitchen at the time of the last strike, with the Touhy bunch tried and are trying their utmost to poison Al with food and contraband candy. Al in turn would not touch same it being that he was told what they were try-ing to do to him, at the present time until I left there last month. There are two others working in the kitchen by the name of Sparky prison #200 and Bob Sheridan #199 which are pretending and making Al feel that they are his friend, waiting for an opportunity to knife or poison him. To be frank with you and make you fully realize the meaning and danger for your brother Al is that he must by all means

get out of there and be sent to another prison.   They have
marked him for his life and it is only matter of time you will
hear the saddest news of your life, knowing beyond a doubt that
his life is at stake.   Being that I was the orchestra leader
and due out May 6th, 1936, a party by the name of Chas. Herta
and McDonald #115 approached me and said unless Al gave me
the O.K. to get them $5000 for an escape plan and forward it
to the following address:

    Mrs. Myrtle Bloxham,
     1717- 4th St.,
      South Bellingham, Washington,

and--

    Mrs. G. Berta,
     129 Filmore St.,
      San Francisco, Calif.,

that they would get Al and that he would never leave there
alive.   I was to get in contact with the following people and
have arrangements made for an escape with said money to be
turned over to these people.

  Thomas Cross, an ex-convict out of McNeil Isl. following
locations to find the above for me to get or write to the
Chaplin of the Christian Science Church at McNeil Island to
receive the add. of the mother on false pretense to be a
friend and to get in personal contact with Thomas Cross,
and for me to give him the outlay of the prison ground and
also the secret signals which will be as follows:

  A fast motor boat with a row-boat behind to go around
the island two days in succession after Berta had a visit

from his wife which she in turn would set the date and time;
I was to see lawyer of San Francisco by name of Nat Coughlin,
he in turn would get me in touch with Berta's wife and for me
to give her plans for escape and for me to write to a convict
now in Leavenworth, Kansas, by name of Dooley Chas., who is
due out soon and knows all the plans, he in turn is a friend
of Thos. Cross and also to the ones in Alcatraz Prison. Said
prisoner received plans and information through a fellow that
was transferred back to Leavenworth, Kansas, about six months
ago by name of Mike.   The previous day of my relase from
Alcatraz I was interviewed by the Deputy warden, called and
brought before him in the show room in regards to these escape
plans which he in turn happens to know all about it. He agrees
with me that Al's life is in danger and would like to see him
transferred out of there.   I don't believe you know the dangers
as Al cannot go out in the yard; it is now going on for the past
year and that he is in real danger with his life. This information is known by all the guards and officials of the Island.
It seems that with all this Al is afraid to eat the food and
his health is failing him.   These facts are the Almighty and
God's truth and all because Al refuses to be a party to these
escape plans and upon it all trying to be a model prisoner.
He has made more enemies by not being in with these plans
and strikes.   It seems and I know and fear things will get
worse when some of these same men get out of solitary
confinement; there are numerous other things such as

burning his clothes week after week from the laundry. It
seems that most of these men threaten Al's life for not send-
ing money to different people, such as this man Jack Baker
who works in blacksmith shop, and said unless receives $500
he will knife or poison Al or get even some dirty mean way.
He wants $500 sent to Mrs. Grant Morrison, 127 North Edgement,
Los Angeles, Calif.

These facts I happen to know as I was music teacher for
Al for 1-1/2 yrs. and knew every move and attempts that have
failed towards his life and constant tortures that he is going
through daily.   After spending half of my life in various
prisons there is none so corrupt as Alcatraz.   I beg of you
as his brother to make these facts known or have me brought
before the proper officials at Washington and confronted with
the Deputy Warden of Alcatraz.   I am sure and feel that Atty.
General would not stand to see Al killed in cold blood when
he has proven himself a model prisoner and helped to better
himself in music.   I know and take solemn oath to the above
facts to be truthful, and it is more serious than I can
explain in writing.

(Signed) Chas. Mangiere #97

One month later, on June 23, 1936, James Lucas, #224, stabbed Capone in the back with half a pair of scissors.

Capone was not seriously hurt, but his family and attorney once again demanded he be transferred. As strongly as before, prison officials refused.

OFFICE OF
CHIEF MEDICAL OFFICER

TREASURY DEPARTMENT

UNITED STATES
PUBLIC HEALTH SERVICE
UNITED STATES PENITENTIARY
ALCATRAZ, CALIFORNIA

June 25, 1936.

Warden Johnston,
Institution,

Sir: Re: CAPONE, Alphonse,   Number 85 -AZ

On June 23, 1936 the above named inmate was brought to the hospital with multiple stab wounds and with a history as follows;

About 9:30 A.M. while engaged at work in the clothing room he was attacked by another inmate with a pair of clothing sdissors. He gave the name Lucas, number 224, as the man who stabbed him. His condition at the time he was brought to the hospital was that of semi-shock. He was given the usual circulatory stimulants and then other first aid measures and an examination.

The primary examination and treatment was given by Doctor Greenberg. He found several wounds as follows; a small punctured wound in the left chest posteriorly about 2 cm. long and 2 cm. deep which did not penetrate the chest cavity, a puntured wound on the medial aspect of the left thumb about 1 1/2 cm. in length and extending to the bone, several superficial wounds - two on the right arm and one on the right hand. Under the flouroscope there was seen a foreign body embedded in the first phalanx of the left thumb. This was removed by operation in the operating room under local anaesthesia, it was the point of a scissor's blade and was about 1/2 inch in length. The piece of blade was strongly embedded in the bone and much difficulty was experienced in removing the object. He was given 1500 units of tetanus antitoxin.

The patient is recovering from the injuries in a satisfactory manner. The prognosis is considered good at this time. He will probably be confined to the hospital for at least three more days.

Respectfully,

George Hess

George Hess, A A Surgeon,
Chief Medical Officer.

Chicago, Illinois,
7244 Prairie Avenue,
June 25, 1936.

Hon. Sanford Bates,
    Director,
        Bureau of Prisons,
            Wasington, D. C.

Dear Mr. Bates:

Referring to our conference this morning relative to our appeal for the transfer of my brother Al from Alcatraz, and confirming my verbal statement to you, I respectfully state that on behalf of myself, Al's wife, and our mother, that we will gladly assume all responsibility for his safety and welfare if you transfer him to one of our other prisons.

Further, in the event of Al being transferred to some other institution, I will personally assume full responsibility and guilt for any bribes of officials or guards, also other prisoners, seeking any special privileges, favors, etc., and, in fact, anything of any nature whatsoever in violation of your prison rules, all of which, I repeat, I will assume full responsibility and the guilt thereof.

The family feels that an immediate transfer is vitally necessary, not only because his life is in danger, but his health is impaired due to his lack of fresh air, exercise, extreme nervous condition, mental worries, because of existing conditions and he cannot enjoy the yard privileges, being at all times fearful of criminal attack.

Thanking you for your kind consideration and trusting that you will transfer him at the earliest possible moment, I beg to remain

Respectfully yours,

Ralph J Capone

Following the attack, life on Alcatraz was relatively quiet for Capone, despite a renewed notoriety in the eyes of the public.

One person tried to send Capone a picture of his dog. Prison officials would not deliver it. Another wanted Capone to join other supposed celebrities in writing a book of funny sayings for tombstones. Again, prison administrators refused on Al's behalf.

US Attorney General Homer Cummings (at left, with cane) walks with Warden James A. Johnston during a formal inspection of the correctional officers.

One woman sent a cryptic letter to Capone along with a check for sixteen octillion dollars ($16,000,000,000,000,000,000,000,000,000.00) signed "Holy Moses." Fearing the correspondence might be some type of code, prison officials asked the Chief Intelligence Unit of the Bureau of Internal Revenue to investigate. Carlos M. Bernstein of the Alcohol Tax Unit was assigned to the case. "Obviously the letter… and the enclosed check," he reported, "are the products of a person lacking proper mental balance, and apparently contained no coded message."

41

9 SEPT 25 MENU 2

RICE & TOMATO SOUP
BAKED MEAT HASH
CATSUP
1 SOFT BOILED EGG
PICKLED CUCUMBERS & ONIONS
SPICED LOAF CAKE
BREAD   COFFEE

All, Golden Gate National Recreation Area/Park Archives

The dining hall, ca. 1937, with a contemporary menu. According to prison records, Capone's advancing illness became apparent one morning while on his way to breakfast. Right, the guard watching the kitchen sat in a glass office, which offered some protection while allowing visibility.

While public attention kept officials jumping, Al himself was beginning to slow down.

Capone's records show that he was a regular visitor to the prison hospital for sitz-baths and nasal problems. But these were minor discomforts compared to those about to take their toll.

February 5, 1938

To: J. A. Johnston, Warden

From: E. J. Miller, Associate Warden

Re: CAPONE, Alphonse   #85-Az

When we opened cells for mess this morning at breakfast time, Capone #85-Az came out of his with his blue clothes on. On being sent back to his cell to put on his coveralls, he returned, put them on and got in line and came in and drank some coffee.

After the meal was over and men went back to cells Capone started up on the upper gallery instead of going to his own cell. Officers sent him back to his own cell and he acted very peculiarly. After entering his own cell and being locked in, he proceeded to get sick and threw up what he had eaten for breakfast and then appeared to be all right.

After we let the men go out to work, I went up to Capone's cell and talked to him to see what was the matter with him and what explanation he had for his actions. He was sitting on the toilet and in response to my questions all I could get were indistinct, incoherent mumblings.

At about 8:15, Mr. Amende, Cell House Officer, called me and said that Capone had thrown a fit in his cell. I went to Capone's cell and found he was laying on the floor and appeared to be in a hysterical fit of some sort. I immediately sent for the Doctor and when Dr. Hess came and put him on the bunk and examined him, he said we had better take him to the Hospital.

Capone was checked into the Hospital.

Years before, Capone had been diagnosed with syphilis, a then-incurable sexually transmitted disease destined to affect both his mind and his body. Al had been treated in Chicago and at Atlanta Penitentiary, but by the time he came to Alcatraz, Al thought he needed no more treatments for his condition.

By this time, Capone had accumulated credit for "good time" and had less than a year left to serve at Alcatraz.

But on February 5, 1938, he began having convulsions. Doctors recognized his symptoms as "paresis," mental deterioration brought on by syphilis affecting the brain. From then on, Capone would never be the same. He soon began exhibiting the unmistakable symptoms of his disease, including skin problems, memory loss, and irrational behavior. News that he was "going crazy" traveled fast, and once again Al found himself in the public eye.

Re: **CAPONE**, Alphonse   # 85-Az

        Attached is interview slip from Alphonse Ca
dated February 10, 1938, reading as follows:

        To: Deputy Warden E. J. Miller
        Sir

        Please grant me an interview regarding
        Will you please give me permission to see you
        Deputy, as I have a few things of importance
        I would like to take up with you in regards
        to what happened to me, and to get myself
        straightened out in everything bad that Ive done,
        to me truthfully, all I can say is I don't
        remember a thing wrong I did, so please see me
        Respectfully   Alphonse Capone #85-Az

        I went to the Hospital and talked to Capone at
12:50 P.M. this date.

        He told me that he did not know what happened, that
it was just like a curtain down over him that day he fell out
in his cell. If he had done anything wrong, he did not mean to.

        He wanted to know if he could have his cell and job
back again when he was O.K. Said he was going to behave and
follow the Doctor's orders.

        He said that Dr. Hess told him that it was broadcasted
and in all the papers that he was crazy. I told him that I did
not know anything about that. He wanted to know if he could
write to his wife and mother. I told him he could in the regular
way and through the regular channels.

        He talked very rationally at all times and seemed
anxious to impress me that he was going to behave in the future

44

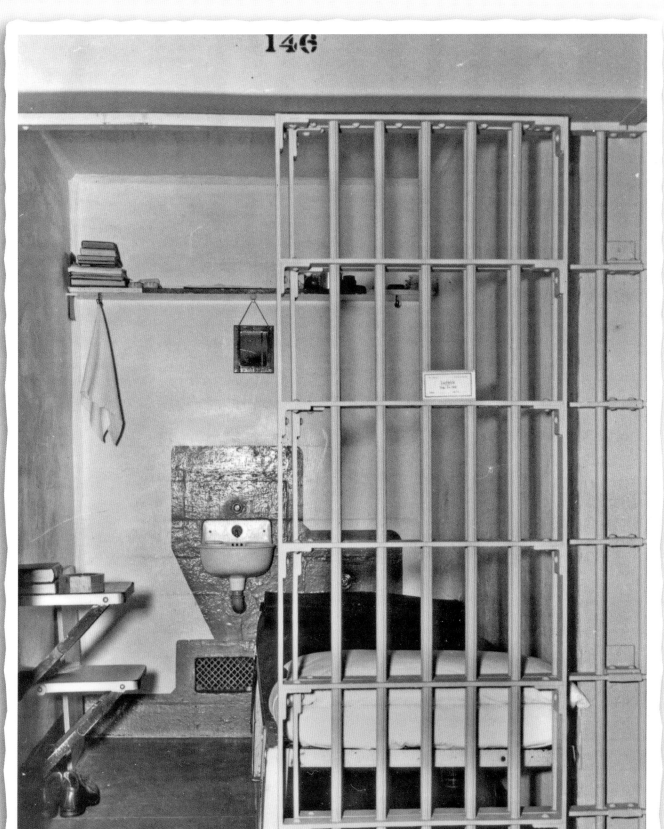

A typical Alcatraz prison cell: 5' wide, 9' deep, 7' tall. Capone began his stay on Alcatraz in cell 433, but was later moved to cell 181, where he spent most of his time on the island. In these early years, few personal effects were allowed.

To Dr. Edward Twitchell
San Francisco, Cal.

If Alcatraz is anything like the Hudson River State
Hospital at Poughkeepsie, N.Y., I don't wonder that
Capone or anyone else would go crazy. After my
experiences at the latter place(dirty low down dump
that it is) I could never forget.

                              Anonymous

His illness made Capone's behavior erratic,
and predictably, reports that he was "going
crazy" soon began appearing in the press.

why fool with that Rat Capone he's only keeping prison. hit him in the head with an ax and dump his rotten carcass, over the wall to the sharks in the ocean. then keep it up with the rest of his ilk until you rid the country of them. why should we pay taxes to keep them. An American

completely
Original - typewritten   no signat...

Warden James Johnston
San Francisco

Sir
      I am one of the for er gang of Capone. If I get caught at
this I will go as the man did yester ay. I want you to know
what it is all about. The gang has it all planned. they have
money plenty, they plan for Capone to act crazy so you will
send him to the mental hospital and then they break him out
as that would be easy up there. They went up and looked it
all ove and they have ade plans. On the Island there is a
man who keeps the outside in touch and they have been planning
for two years. You see he asked again for pardon and it was
refused, this is the way how to get him out and each one is
promised plenty and then they go to o America.

      I am now working and out of it all but have way to find
out. He is dangerous and controls so many you should be able to
get enough on him to keep him in for life. he knows about
the Lindbergh gang on the snatch and he could tell you plenty
about Arnold of N.Y. and a few others money did it all and he
has lots put away in different parts under other names.

      Watch close, if this does not work there is a plan to
make a break at the Island. The two who got away were the
start they are now on the coast in disguise you could easly pick
them up if the federals got on it good. they have map
of island and know the entire set.

                              Frisky

Envelope postmarked Philadelphia, Pa 4 Feb 14 11-PM 1938
addressed to Warden James Johnston

From then on, Capone stayed in the prison hospital, where doctors tried to find a way to treat him.

With the development of penicillin still years away, little could be done to address Al's condition. Desperate, he finally agreed to a radical new treatment.

A decade before, in 1927, Austrian neurologist Julius Wagner-Jauregg had won the Nobel Prize in Medicine for his discovery that high fevers sometimes improved the condition of patients with neurological symptoms from syphilis. He injected patients with malaria to induce these therapeutic fevers, and then controlled the malaria with quinine.

That's how prison officials tried to help Al Capone: They inoculated him with malaria in the hopes that the fevers would improve his condition. But it didn't work.

The Ethical Society,
Davenport, Iowa.

Davenport, Iowa,
Feb. 10 / 38.

Mr.James A.Johnston,Warden,
Alcatraz Prison,
San Francisco,Cal.

Dear Mr.Johnston:

As we read about the Ex-Gangster on Rampage,in our local paper,with his picture with a cigar in his mouth," Going Mad,"we are wondering and the question is being asked: Does the state furnish cigars and matches to these criminals ?

When we realize that smoking,at best,is a bad habit that should not be encouraged in good society,it is amazing to see etequete violated in a penal institution .

Please explain and oblige,

Very truly yours,

John F.Bredow

John F.Bredow, S

Ethical Society .

TREASURY DEPARTMENT
U. S. PUBLIC HEALTH SERVICE
Form 1946 G
Sept., 1927

CLINICAL RECORD

WARD SURGEON'S PROGRESS AND TREATMENT RECORD

Ward surgeons will record on this sheet the diet, treatment, complications, changes of diagnosis, intercurrent diseases, and daily progress of the case, and will initial each notation.

DATE	DIET	TREATMENT	DAILY NOTES
		This morning the patient is smiling, talks c̄ same dysarthria and seems somewhat confused. The pupils are typically Argyll Robertson. Seen by Dr Fritchell. GH	
		3 P.M. Patient is prowling about the small ward and out into the hallway. Place pt in observation cell ?. GH	
2-7-38.	Reg.	Patient doesn't eat his food. Says he just doesn't care for any. Had a very restless night. Asked several times if his son was all right. Has a silly grin on face. Made and remade his bed several times during the night. Seems somewhat disoriented as to time and place. Very pleasant but is beginning to get a little boisterous. GH.	
2-8-38	Mid Nite.	Patient has been awake all evening and has been yelling, singing and laughing in a silly childish manner. He has also been throwing himself under the bed and also trying to mimic some of June's escapades in the next cell. He stands in front of his cell door with the bed linen across	

July 15, 1938.

J:

To The Warden and Chief Medical Officer,
Alcatraz, California.

It is my wish that I be given the Malarial Treatment
for Neuro-Syphilis if and when it is decided by you that such
treatment is indicated as offering some hope of further
improvement in my condition. I make this request in full
knowledge of the nature of the treatment requested and
without any urging on the part of anyone.

Respectfully,

Alphonse Capone

Alphonse Capone, № 85-Az.

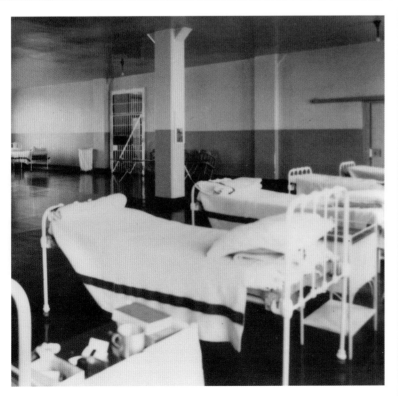

As Capone's health deteriorated, he began spending more and more time in the prison hospital (left). This letter records Capone's agreement to try a newly available medical treatment. Opposite, a page from the hospital's daily log; note that on 2-7-38, Capone repeatedly made and unmade his bed. This type of odd behavior, which recurred during his illness, was widely reported by the press.

UNITED STATES PENITENTIARY
ALCATRAZ, CALIFORNIA

CONDUCT REPORT

NAME ___CAPONE, Alphonse___   No.___85-AZ___

DATE REPORTED	OFFENSE AND ACTION
10-10-34	TALKING IN LINE OF MARCH. This prisoner was talking in line this PM with Collins-#208. This prisoner knows better and has been warned. GUARD NELSON. Action:To lose two weeks yard privileges. C.J.Shuttleworth, Deputy
12-19-34	UNNECESSARY NOISE AT THE TABLE. Caused confusion in the mess hall after meal was finished. GUARD W.B.COTTERAL. Action: To forfeit one weeks yard privileges. C.J.Shuttleworth, Deputy Warden
2-20-35	FIGHTING IN THE LAUNDRY. This prisoner had a fight with Colyer-185 while working in the laundry. He did not resist when I separated them. Some of the prisoners claim he had been doing a lot of bullying lately over the other prisoners who work with him. GUARD- I.B. FAULK. Action: Placed in solitary confienment restricted diet and forfeit all privileges until further orders. C.J. Shuttleworth, Deputy Warden
2-28-35	Removed from solitary to segregations
3-2-35	Removed to regular cell & work assignment, privileges restored. C.J. Shuttleworth, Deputy Warden
5-24-35	SPITTING ON THE FLOOR. While waiting on the range, out side of cell, to be let into his cell, Capone expectorated on the floor, flats, and cell house wall; he left the library about three minutes before and there is no cause for such filthy action. GUARD P.A. HABOUSH. Action:To lose two weeks yard privileges. C.J. Shuttleworth, Deputy Warden.
6-3-35	CONVERSING WITH #43-WALSH. Thsi inmate was talking at cell door with Walsh in adjoining cell. Both men ducked inside when I appeared. GUARD P.A. HABOUSH. Action: Reprimanded and Warned. C.J.Shuttleworth, Deputy.
9-5-35	ENTERING CELL BEFORE SIGNAL. While marching to the cells from evening meal, this man entered his cell instead of stopping at the door and wait for the signal to enter. GUARD NEELEY. Action: Reprimanded & Warned. C.J. Shuttleworth, Deputy Warden.
9-18-35	WASTING FOOD. Eating the center of piece of cake and leaving the balance on his plate. GUARD J.B. STEERE. Action: To lose breakfast, 9/19/35, C. J. Shuttleworth, Deputy Warden.
4-21-36	FIGHTING WITH #257-HENSLEY. I answered the buzzer for hospital and found #85 and #257 fighting. Mr. Preshaw and I parted them. Mr. Ping witnessed start of agument upstairs. M.A. AMENDE, Jr. Officer
11-11-38	CREATING DISTURBANCE, DESTROYING CLOTHING, Upon being told that he could not go to the yard, this prisoner flew into a rage, kicking the door and cursing evryone. He destroyed his blue uniform and bath robe and threw them over the transom into hall. He kept this up for about one hour. Report #2231, R. L. King, Junior Officer. Action: To forfeit show privileges this date. E. J. Miller, Associate Warden.

FPI ! C—FLK—9-11-36—500—791C-87

Records show that Al got into a few fights, and once (in 1935), ended up in solitary confinement. The issue behind the 1938 disturbance most likely had its genesis in Capone's advancing illness. Above and left, Capone, Colyer, Walsh, and Hensley.

Officers patrolled catwalks from which they could observe the area in and around the prison. This guard tower, ca. 1938, overlooked the dock area. Following page, correctional officer standing in corridor between B and C Block, ca. 1939.

Al's mental and physical condition continued to deteriorate.

He began getting into fights with people in the prison hospital, and threw fits when he didn't get what he wanted. On one day he compulsively made and unmade his bed over and over again; on another day, he threw a bedpan, hitting a man in the head as they fought over Capone's insistence on cleaning the bedpan with a kitchen towel.

Once again, the Capone family wanted Al moved to a prison with a better hospital. As usual, the Bureau of Prisons declined. Al spent the next eleven months in the hospital at Alcatraz, his physical and mental health steadily declining.

Capone was released from Alcatraz in January 1939, but he couldn't go home just yet. He still owed one more year in prison for a contempt of court sentence he'd received in 1932, when he'd failed to show up for a Cook County, Illinois, grand jury investigation.

Since the prospect of bringing Capone back to the Chicago area did not appeal to the Cook County authorities, he was sent instead to the Terminal Island Federal Prison facility near Long Beach, California.

December 18th

To My Dear Wife:

"Well dear heart of mine, here is your dear husband, who loves you, with all my heart and soul. First thanks for all your lovely letters this month. Sure glad to read the good news, that you and our dear love, are in perfect health. I just came back from church, Father Clark had another priest here, who just came back from Italy, and he gave us a good sermon all about Italy and Germany. In the mean time dear heart of mine please do not worry about me, as I am improving every day. I get two treatments a week and they do not hurt me at all. I work out in the recreation yard five days a week, and Saturday and Sunday I catch up on my music and read a number of Monthly and Weekly Magazines, and a hot bath every day, and three good meals each day. I hope to see you and Sonny again before I leave here next January the 18th. I have quite a number of songs written for him to sing them to you, and I will play them on the piano or my Mandola.

"Yes dear I had a nice letter from Sonny dated Dec. 3rd, and he told me that the 20th of this month he will be 20 years old. Yes Sweet, he is sure a Son to be proud of, and from the day I come home, he, you, and I will sure go to town in regards to our happiness. I intend to spend the rest of my life, right there in Palm Island, and you and Son and I will get plenty of happiness for our future. We seen a lovely picture on Thanksgiving day, and we will have another one next Christmas. Yes Dear, next Saturday I go to Confession and the following Sunday we will get Communion, and my prayers will be all for you two. In the meantime thank all of my family for all their lovely letters and give them all my love. Get in touch with my dear brother Ralph, and for him to arrange to pay that $37,000 fine and costs I have to pay here, And when I go to the County Jail I will have to pay another fine there of $10,000. But when I come there I can see you, and hon, and all of our dear family every week and when I'm through with that Sentence, never again, will I ever do anything that will keep me away from you, and Hon. tell him to continue with his golf playing, as I intend to play with him every day and nights, the three of us will see either a Movie or a show or go to one of our own night clubs and dance all of troubles away. I now weight 204, and feel fine and dandy, and when you come here on the next visit, bring me a picture of Sonny, you, and his Sweetheart. Tell Ralph not to worry about me, as I'm satisfied with everything here and hope to see him as soon as I come to Chicago. Love and Kisses to you and Sonny,

Your Dear Husband Alphonse Capone #85"

xxxxxxxxxxxxxxx

UNITED STATES BUREAU OF PRISONS

INTRA-BUREAU CORRESPONDENCE

Federal Correctional Institution
Terminal Island, California
January 9, 1939

TO: Mr. James V. Bennett, Director

RE: Transfer of Alphonse Capone, No. 397-Cal.

IN REPLY REFER TO:

The reason that I have not written before in reference to receiving Capone is that I have been awfully busy trying to keep the newspapers and different ones from getting any information pertaining to Capone.

Warden Johnston called me on Friday evening around 6:30 o'clock notifying me of the train and car Capone would be on. Ever since my return from up north I have been living here at the institution so that I could be close by waiting for this movement, as I did not know when it would take place.

I drove my personal car up to Glendale to meet Capone and the officers, thereby avoiding any publicity. We arrived at the institution and had Capone checked in by 9:45 A.M. Immediately after Associate Warden Miller called Warden Johnston on the long distance phone, the Associated Press and other papers started calling about Capone.

The papers have not received any information from me in reference to Capone, as I have referred them to you for any statement. Quite naturally there have been articles in the different papers quoting me but none of these are correct.

In Capone's first letter to his wife he stated, "If I am not out by the 19th, you will know there is something wrong." I asked Capone what he meant by this and told him that more than likely he would be here for another year or so. After my conversation with him he asked if he could rewrite the letter, which I allowed him to do. In this letter, which was mailed to his wife today, he has informed her that he wants to do his other year at this place as he likes it. This is just for your information.

Enclosed are a few of the clippings taken from the different papers.

E. J. LLOYD,
W A R D E N.

At Terminal Island, Capone's condition went from bad to worse.

Confused and belligerent, Capone started so many fights that he was not allowed out in the yard with other prisoners. His schedule was set up to ensure that he came into contact with as few people as possible. His work detail — at one point, cleaning a trash platform — was done when everyone else was in the yard. When the prisoners returned to their cells, Capone reported to the prison hospital. Once again, Al got credit for "good time" served and was released early, in November 1939.

Administrative
Form No. 16
May, 1937

UNITED STATES BUREAU OF PRISONS
INTRA-BUREAU CORRESPONDENCE
Federal Correctional Institution.

Terminal Island, Calif.
Jan.11, 1939

TO:Warden-U.S.P.Alcatraz, Calif.

RE:Perosnal property of Alphonse Capone.

IN REPLY REFER TO: Record Office.

Re: Our-Alponse Capone-Reg. No.397-Cal

Your-   "   "   Reg. No. 85-Az

The following personal property of the above named inmate

received.

93 Photos

1 String of rosary beads

1 Leather case

5 Religious medals

5 Letters

3 Letters (copies)

1 Telegram(copy)

4 Greeting cards

5 Religious photos.

U. S. PENITENTIARY
ALCATRAZ ISLAND, CALIF.
REC'D

JAN 16 1939

Signed

C.G.Weaver, Record Clerk.

NO. 397-CAL
TERMINAL ISLAND

Courtesy Michael Esslinger

This Terminal Island mug shot is sometimes misidentified as Capone as a teenager; the facial lesions were a symptom of his illness.

APPOINTED
HOTEL

TELEPHONE 473
TELEGRAMS
CRANFORD HOTEL
LITTLEHAM CROSS
EXMOUTH

The CRANFORD HOTEL

RESIDENT PROPRIETORS
MR.& MRS.CORDEN GILBERT.

LITTLEHAM CROSS
EXMOUTH
DEVON

12th April 1939.

The Governor,
Alcatraz Prison.
Alcatraz Island.
U.S,A.

Sir,

I am taking the liberty of writing to you and
asking you if you would oblige me by obtaining a signature
of one of the inmates of your Prison, namely"Scarface"
Al Capone.

I have a collection of autographs of quite high
standard and do not think it will be complete without the
signature of a notorious criminal, so I have chosen Al Capone,
America's Public Enemy No. 1.

My chief reason in writing this letter is to
obtain your autograph also, as you must be a man of renowned
character, to be able to control such criminals.

Yours faithfully,

Edward Corden-Gilbert,

56

August 23, 1939

Patient was interviewed by Dr. Smith, consulatant psychiatrist. He spoke at great length of how he had broken up the strike at Alcatraz, of his difficulties with Blacky Adell, and of what he would do when he got out. He was going to build four factories, two for furniture and two for autos, and was now going to employ 25,000 to 50,000 people.

August 21, 1939

Patient has not been living up to his schedule and had to be brought in twice from the yard this morning. He argued that no one else knew how to take care of the handball courts.

August 20, 1939

Patient had to be taken in off the yard today. He became excited while watching the wrestling match and believed that one of the wrestlers was biting the other in earnest. He finally quieted down.

August 16, 1939

Patient states that he is now satisfied to remain on his present assignment. He states with pride that he fixed the ball courts and cleaned the walks well yesterday.

August 17, 1939

Special Reducing Diet.

Breakfast:
 Cereal with milk
 Fruit
 Two eggs, two strips bacon
 1 slice toast
 coffee
Lunch:
 One salad
 One glass (cup) milk
 One glass fruit juice
Supper:
 One steak
 Two vegetables
 One slice bread, 1 piece b
 One glass milk

Hot tub bath (15 minutes, a
by tepid shower.

Potassium Iodide min. XV b.i
min. XXX b.i.d.

Record weight daily.

A page from the prison hospital record reveals Al's physical and mental state while at Terminal Island. Below, brother (Ralph) and mother (Theresa), during a 1939 visit to Al at Terminal Island. Because Ralph was a convicted felon, he was not allowed to visit Al during his Alcatraz incarceration.

CAPONE, Alphonso

FORMAL PSYCHOLOGICAL EXAMINATION AS OF AUGUST 30th, 1939:

By the revised Stanford Binet intelligence test he has a mental of eight years and eleven months placing him in the middle-grade moron group. He showed scatter from the eight to thirteen year levels on the test. His answers to questions well illustrate his thought content.

Q. "What ought you to do before undertaking something very important"?

A. "Make sure you don't violate any laws and that you won't cause anyone any grief".

Q. "Why should we judge a person more by his actions than his word"?

A. "Make sure he does something out of the way then critize him".

Q. "What is the difference between a President and a King"?

A. "We can't have Kings in the United States. Roosevelt runs the United States, Kings run Europe. You can change a King any time according to public opinion. The King gets to office by big millionaires who control the country".

Q. "What is the difference between idleness, and laziness"?

A. "One fellow is lazy and won't do anything, the other fellow just won't do any work".

Q. "What is the difference between poverty and misery"?

A. "Poverty is when you ain't got nothing to make you happy. Misery is when you ain't got nothing and no place to sleep".

Q. "What is the difference between character and reputation"?

A. "If you do things in the good world then naturally everyone knows you did good, thats character. You either do good or bad whatever your reputation is. When I made my first big money I took care of my family and opened soup kitchens. I gave the poor three meals a day. The Hearst papers branded me as no-good. My friends knew I was just the opposite. I made a mistake but committed no crime. I wanted to pay my taxes in 1932 but they wouldn't take my money".

Q. "Whats wrong with this? The Judge said to the prisoner you are to be hanged and I hope it will be a warning to you".

A. "The Judge thinks he is doing the right thing by giving warning"?

Q. "What is wrong with this? A well known railroad had its last accident five years ago, and since that time it has killed one person in a collision".

A. "Its a good railroad. Railroads now have accidents daily".

Q. "Whats wrong with this? When there is a collision the last car of the train is usually damaged the most. So they have decided that it will be best if the last car is always taken off before the train starts".

A. "Its according how severe the collision is".

Continued -

58

CAPONE, Alphonso (cont'd)

Q. "What is wrong with this? Bill Jones feet are so big that he has to pull his trousers on over his head".
A. "His trousers are too big".
Q. "Whats funny about this? A man called one day at the Post-office and asked if they was a letter waiting for him. What is your name asked the Postmaster? Why said the man, you will find my name on the envelope".
A. "He should have told the Postmaster his name so that he wouldn't have any trouble finding the letter".
Q. "What is funny about this? The fireman hurried to the burning house, got his fire-hose ready, and after smoking a cigar put out the fire".
A. "He was satisfied and smoked a cigar".
Q. "What is funny about this? In an old graveyard in Spain they have discovered a small skull which they believe is that of Christopher Columbus when he was ten years old".
A. "How could they prove it was Christopher Columbus".
Q. "What is funny about this? One day we saw several icebergs that had been entirely melted by the warmth of the Gulf streams".
A. "Icebergs don't come where the Gulf streams is".

Chief
Medical
Officer
- - - -

HOSPITAL
***
M E M O R A N D U M
A u g u s t 18th 1939

O.H.Cronacher
S t e w a r d

Please furnish the Hospital with the following;

1 lb Bacon

1 Steak daily until further notice

Harry R. Lipton, A.A.Surgeon
Acting Chief Medical Officer

Dr. Lipton;
  Please defer the diet
on Capone until we
have a chance to talk
it over again.
              G.H.

Opposite, a psychological examination reveals how much Capone's cognitive abilities had declined; Doctors Harry Lipton and George Hess (G.H.) work out Capone's "special diet." Hess had been Capone's doctor at Alcatraz. Following page, Terminal Island prison, 1938.

Examiner's Report

TO: Chief Medical Officer

Patient's Name:- CAPONE, Alphonse
                 Reg. No. 397-Cal

PSYCHIATRIC EXAMINATION:

September 9th 1939

    This patient has been under the care of the examiner since
August 1st 1939, and has been seen several times daily. He has
a flushed appearance and is somewhat untidy in personal habits.
During interviews he is friendly and ingratiating. He smiles
constantly and at intervals winks and nods his head in approval
and satisfaction. He seals all promises with a handshake and
usually shakes hands on departing.

    Speech is under moderate pressure and he leads all conver-
sations. His productions are repetitious and somewhat rambling
with not infrequent conflicting statements. They show much egoism
and grandiose ideas. His mood has been characterized by mild euphoria.
No frank delusions or hallucinations have been elicited. His thoughts
center chiefly about his wife and son, and the approaching reunion
with them. Altrustic ideals are repeatedly expressed. He states
that he has under construction two factories in Miami and that he
is planning to eventually complete four in which he will manufacture
automobiles and furniture. He states that he will employ ex-convicts;
"one-time losers," who got into difficulty because of extenuating cir-
cumstances. He will build homes on the grounds for employees with
families and apartments for single employees. He repeatedly makes
reference to soup kitchens he allegedly operated in Chicago during
the depression and relates many anecdotes to impress upon the examiner that his heart is with the poor and downtrodden. He has asked
to be allowed to work in the library but this has been discouraged.
He is correctly oriented. Sensorial examination reveals impairment
of the higher associative processes. His remote memory is fairly
good. Recent memory however is defective in part.

    He has been receiving treatment consisting of iodides, orally;
tryparsamide, intravenously and bismuth, intramuscularly. Patient
wrote daily interviews to officials requesting work changes.

cont'd

Examiner's Report
To Chief Medical Officer
Re: CAPONE, Alphonse
    Reg. No. 397-Cal

P a g e 2 -

Patient had a mild upset on the evening of August the third. He
pounded upon the door of his room and shouted to the inmate in
the next room to "keep quiet." His daily activities were regulated
on August 17th, when he was permitted yard privileges mornings
and afternoons following which he received hydrotherapy.   He
frequently found excuses to disrupt his schedule. Patient was
upset August 9th in the recreation hall, when he says one of the
men made some noise while the radio was playing. Patient states
he reprimanded that individual. His condition was discussed with
him following which he promised to walk away from all unpleasant
situations, avoid entanglements and consult the examiner. Patient
had to be taken off the yard the afternoon of August 20th. He
became excited while watching a wrestling match and believed that
one of the wrestlers was biting the other in earnest. August 21st
he was brought in twice from the yard. As a defense he stated that
no one else knew how to take care of the handball courts. August
23rd he was interviewed by Doctor Smith, Consultant Psychiatrist.
He spoke at great length about how he had broken up the strike
at Alcatraz and of his difficulties with "Blackie" Odell, and of
what he would do when he got out. He stated that he was going to
build four factories and employ 25 to 50 thousand people. August
24th he wrote an interview to the Warden asking to be removed from
the hospital and placed in a dormitory. He also requested a job
working on the reservation. His condition was discussed with at
some length whereupon he agreed to continue with his present pro-
gram and desist from writing daily interview slips to officials.
September 2nd the patient related, with some pride, how he had
struck Erunes, number 735, in the face with his fist and kicked
him, throwing him against the table when the latter was preparing
to assault Ponce, number 787, with a fork, after Erunes had knocked
Ponce down. As a result of the assault by Capone, Erunes sustained
a laceration of the occiput which necessitated suturing. September
7th, patient assaulted Herlihy, number 476, (hospital attendant),
after the latter had closed his door. This attendant has been in-
structed to close all doors in the Annex while the "sick-line" is
being held. The assault was without provocation. Patient struck
Herlihy in the face knocking him to the floor. When Herlihy arose
and asked patient what was wrong, patient struck him several more
blows, throwing him to the floor again. According to patient,
Herlihy called him a "Dago Son of a b - -." According to attendants
and other inmates, however, Herlihy had not spoken to patient.
Patient was seen in his room and was told that he was going to
segregation. Thereupon he became enraged. He stated that officials
did not want him to go home, that he might as well commit suicide
and that he was going to do so. He picked up a comb from his bed
and scratched both sides of his throat. He resisted being placed
in segregation and had to be assisted by several custodial officers.

cont'd

There he struck his head against the wall and threatened to
gouge his eyes out. He was undressed and given a blanket to
keep warm. He was abusive in language and raved loudly for
about 15 minutes following which he quieted down and accepted
a swab to paint his neck. The morning of September 8th he
stated that he would henceforth behave and asked to be released
from segregation. He stated that it was "commissary day" and
he had to buy "supplies" for Belty, Clark and Steele, all of
whom were "good boys." He was told the matter would be taken
up with other officials. The evening of September 8th, Kitchner,
a cardiac patient, under strict bed-rest, related that on August
28th he had asked patient, who was passing his room, to get him
a slice of bread. Kitchner stated that patient told him to
"go f - - yourself" and spit in his face. Kitchner alleges
that the following day patient came in his room and began
tickling his toes. He told patient to stop and reminded him of
what happened the night previously, whereupon, patient slapped
him in the face and hit him a severe blow in the abdomen, caus-
ing him to vomit up his supper. Kitchner states that he was
afraid to give this information while patient was on the ward
but is now not fearful as patient is in isolation.

SUMMARY

       This patient has been given every opportunity to adjust
in this institution and has remained poorly cooperative and
viciously assaultive. He presents neurological, pyschological
and psychiatric evidence of general paresis, exspansive-grandiose
type, with marked deterioration. For the safety of the patients
and other inmates detention in isolation is recommended. He
will be allowed on the yard, with another assaultive patient,
when accompanied by a custodial officer.

(September 13th) During the past 4 days patient has been friendly
and ingratiating in manner and has made numerous requests to be
removed from segregation.

Harry R. Lipton
A.A.Surgeon

October 30, 1939

MEMORANDUM FOR THE ATTORNEY GENERAL:

Re: Al Capone

I have received some further information concerning
Al Capone's present attitudes, which may be of interest to you.

The following is quoted from a letter from Dr. George
Hess, the Medical Officer who has been in charge of Capone's
case for sometime. Capone has a genuine regard for Dr. Hess,
and I believe would describe his true feelings to the Doctor.

"He (Capone) has no use for William
Randolph Hearst and threatens to expose him
in his (Capone's) own newspapers, the Cicero
Tribune and the Miami Times. Other than that
he makes no other threats toward Mr. Hearst.
He brands Hearst as a degenerate and claims
that Hearst is the one who is the cause of
all the adverse publicity in his case. He
then makes the remark that Hearst will not
bother him again because they have run him
out of the country and have sold his papers.

"Capone is also bitter toward Judge
Wilkinson (Judge who sentenced him) because
he 'double-crossed' him. In this connection
he does not make any threatening remarks.

"In his present mental state I would
hesitate to place any confidence in any
threats he might make. Since talking to his
brother John and his wife today I believe I
have impressed them with the necessity of
keeping the patient's activities suppressed
at all times. They were both very pleased with
the manner in which you are handling the case
and expressed their gratitude for what I have
done. They did not tell him the plans for the
future and I think they did right because of

the officer present. I have told him that
the plans were to place him in a private
Institution for awhile and he is very
pleased about it."

Warden Lloyd, who also knows Capone quite well,
informed me that Capone is still very bitter against Mr. Hearst
and refers frequently to the occasion when he visited the home
of Mr. Hearst at San Simeon and saw some "carrousing" on the
part of the men and women at the party, which he thought
disgusting. This is the same incident about which he told me
personally. Warden Lloyd thinks also that his bitterness and
threats toward Mr. Hearst are really not dangerous. It is my
own personal feeling, however, that one never can tell what a
paretic will do because it is characteristic of the disease to
rob a man entirely of his judgment.

We have the detailed neuro-psychiatric record on
Capone in the office, which covers about thirty pages. If you
have time to examine it, I should be glad to forward it.

Dr. Fuller, our Medical Director, has had a conference
with Dr. Moore of Johns Hopkins, and it looks as though
Dr. Moore would accept Capone as a patient on condition that
if Capone cannot successfully be treated in the general medical
ward, he will consent to commitment to the Sheppard-Pratt
Hospital for mental cases, which is in Baltimore. This is, as
you may perhaps know, one of the finest institutions in the
country for mental afflictions.

JVB/te

This memo from Bureau of Prisons director
James V. Bennett (JVB) recounts a conversation
between Capone and Chief Medical Officer Hess
in which Al expresses contempt for newspaper
magnate William Randolph Hearst (shown here
with his mistress, actress Marion Davies), whom
Al claimed to have visited.

Capone Prepares to Be Florida Squire

Los Angeles Evening Herald Express 11/3/39

Al Capone, the pudgy Socilian who ruled the Chicago underworld in the heyday of prohibition prepared today to leave Federal prison at Terminal Island and take up life again as the squire of a Florida estate.

All that stands in the way of his release after serving an 11-year sentence with legally deducted credits for good behavior, is the payment of about $10,000 in tax liens. His release has been set officially for Nov. 19, and it was expected that the $10,000 would be made available on that day.

Deputy United States Attorney Maurice Norcop said today:

"Al is in a good humor and probably won't make any fuss and will pay up and leave the prison. The next thing you'll hear of him will be that he is down at his Florida home."

His Irish wife, Mae Capone, and their son are expected to join Capone at the Florida winter home acquired when he was czar of the Chicago underworld.

He is expected to lead a quiet life in Florida. He will be practically a prisoner in his own home. He suffers from paresis, is partially paralyzed and has a great "fear complex" that some of his Chicago enemies will "catch up with him."

Above, his appearance belying reports of his illness, a dapper Capone confers with his lawyer, Abe Teitelbaum, in 1939. Below, Capone's oceanfront estate near Miami, Florida.

TELEGRAM

OFFICIAL BUSINESS—GOVERNMENT RATES

DEPARTMENT OF JUSTICE

DEPARTMENT OF JUSTICE
DIVISION OF RECORDS
TELEGRAPH OFFICE

1939 NOV 3 PM 6:49

DI 29 71 JUS CHICAGO ILLS NOV 3 1939 356P.

J V BENNETT WASHN DC.

ABRAHAM TEITELBAUM ATTORNEY FOR ALPHONSE CAPONE PAID TODAY TWENTY THOUSAND DOLLARS PAYMENTS ACCOUNTS NUMBERS THIRTEEN AND EIGHTEEN RECEIVED TWO CASHIER CHECKS ON THE CHICAGO CITY BANK AND TRUST CO ONE FOR FIVE THOUSAND DOLLARS AND THE OTHER FOR FIFTEEN THOUSAND DOLLARS THE LATTER CHECK MARKED PAID UNDER PROTEST THIS COMPLETES PAYMENT OF ALL FINES AND COST IN CASE NUMBERS TWO THREE TWO THREE TWO AND TWO TWO EIGHT FIVE TWO CONSOLIDATED.

HOYT KING CLERK.

FILE
NOV 4 1939
Bureau of Prisons

DIR
NOV - 4 1939
BUREAU OF PRISONS

642P.

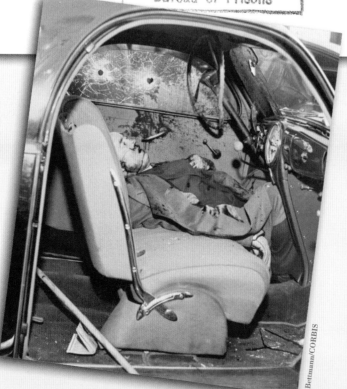

Edward O'Hare, who provided information that helped convict Capone, was murdered just a few days before Capone's release from prison. Years later, Chicago's primary airport was named for his son "Butch," a pilot and WWII hero.

© Bettmann/CORBIS

| Capone (right) and his last lawyer, Abe Teitelbaum, leave the church on Sonny's wedding day.

From Terminal Island, Capone went on to the federal prison at Lewisburg, Pennsylvania. After one day there, he was taken by car to a secret rendezvous near Gettysburg, and was then transferred to another car that took him to nearby Johns Hopkins Medical Center.

In the end, no hospital could help Capone.

Suffering the mental and physical ravages of advanced syphilitic infection, he spent the rest of his life at home.

There, the public saw him enjoying what seemed to be the good life, but his condition never improved. Ultimately, Al had a stroke and developed pneumonia.

At home in Miami, ca. 1945: Al fishing off his dock; posing with wife Mae (left) and her sister Muriel (right), and relaxing with his mother.

On January 25, 1947, at the age of 48,

Alphonse Gabriel Capone quietly died, hidden from the press
in a guest room at his family's Florida mansion.

On February 4, 1947, Al Capone was laid to rest in Chicago's Mount Olivet Cemetery, where his father Gabriel and brother Frank were also interred. The gravesite became a tourist attraction, and following his mother's death in 1952, Capone's body was moved to Mount Carmel, to his mother's plot.

al capone

TRANSFERRED TO FEDERAL CORRECTIONAL INSTITUTION,
TERMINAL ISLAND, CALIFORNIA, JANUARY 6, 1939 (1-6-39)

Commitment & Transfer authority delivered to terminal
island institution at time of transfer of prisoner.

Central file mailed (Registered Mail) to Federal Correctional
Institution, January 9, 1939.

Died in Miami,
Florida
1-25-47